The
Parables
of
Sunlight

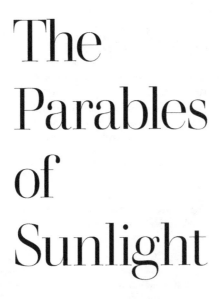

The Parables of Sunlight

Margaret Dulaney

LISTEN WELL PUBLISHING

Paintings by Glenn Harrington

Edited by Aina Barten
Copy edited by Hayden Saunier
Book design by Brooke Koven

ISBN 978-0-9986023-3-2

FIRST PRINTING, 2020

Allie,

Happy,

Tater,

Cotton,

Dolly,

Molly,

Prince

Lyla,

Sweet Pea,

Hibbs,

Tuffy,

Doc,

Angel

Tinker,

Loco,

Otis,

Doodad

With special thanks to Dr. John O'Mahony VMD

The
Parables
of
Sunlight

One

I F I WERE the keeper of a diary—which I am not, having attempted it only once in my life to discover, much to my horror, my inner whiney-pants—but, if I did indulge in the scribbling of daily musings, my entries from some point near the end of the first decade of the twenty-first century would read something like this...

MONDAY:

Visited Allie, the horse, bearing copious amounts of carrots. Redecorated stall (a euphemism for an activity requiring a pitch-fork). Bawled myself dry.

TUESDAY:

Went to visit the horse. Administered massive amounts of carrots. Rearranged stall (note euphemism above). Released remaining eyeball liquids.

WEDNESDAY:

Went to visit horse. Refurbished stall (soon I will come to the bottom of these euphemisms). Discovered hidden stores of tear duct fluid.

THURSDAY:

Horse. Carrots. Euphemism. Tears.

My horse, Allie, has a fractured leg.

IT HAPPENED while nobody was looking (well, no one on two legs). During a mild day in mid-September, as Allie grazed in the pasture with her friends, one of those friends kicked her. I use the word friend here without apology. Horses have such uncanny, co-dependent relationships that ten seconds after being hammered they are known to cry out for their hammerer's company.

Allie had entered my life five years earlier with two very distinctive characteristics: a perfectly etched white heart adorning her forehead (which symbol and its positioning might explain a certain tendency toward oversensitivity) and a trying habit of securing the absolute bottom level of all equine pecking orders. If a horse were going to be picked on, that horse would be Allie.

I took Allie on rather reluctantly—I have always had an intimate relationship with doubt.

The powers of doubt are like mosquitoes, I have found. They wander about aimlessly until they come upon a warm body whose presence incites them to swarm and suck the blood out of their hapless victim. I have tried a number of popular repellents, but none that I can unequivocally recommend.

The warmth that attracts these powers is generated by surety, or so it has seemed for me. Whenever I am most sure of a choice, whenever I have a feeling that almost resembles conviction, doubt rushes in with as much vigor as the initial inspiration and attempts to throttle the certainty right out of me.

This has been such a repetitive phenomenon that I wonder whether the pattern might be universal for those, like me, who are particularly bothered by doubt.

Taking on the responsibility of an off-the-track racehorse in my late forties challenged all the squeaky little voices of doubt that I have wrestled with for much of my life.

MY HUSBAND and I lived in Manhattan for eighteen years before we moved to the rural landscape of Bucks County, Pennsylvania. We had purchased the house several years earlier but made the change of allegiance to our country home in the mid-nineties, trading the clanging of city living for the hooting of owls, the purring of insects. It was the adoption of a new puppy that had convinced us of the need for this move. Her name was Happy, and she was to open the sunlit door for a menagerie of animals whose needs and peculiarities have had much influence on the direction of our lives.

One of the practices that Happy was to convince me that I could not live without was my morning walk. I am sure that without this daily routine you would not be reading this book. I wouldn't have written it. I wouldn't have picked up the pen to write down my thoughts on faith if I hadn't discovered those thoughts in the woods. My friend Sarah tells me that she read somewhere that for the mind the act of walking is like shaking a snow globe. It stirs our thoughts. Charles Dickens was known to walk twenty-five miles a day. George MacDonald writes of the benefits of walking in every one of his novels.

Walking is curative. It can heal both the mind and the body. I have walked myself through frustrations, sorrows, heartaches. I have walked myself out of despair and into joy, past resistance and into acceptance, through chaos and into calm. Europeans seem to value this form of mental and physical therapy more than Americans do. In Switzerland almost the entire population goes hiking on the weekends, from two-year-olds to those in their nineties. There is a network of paths throughout that country that will allow one to walk anywhere one wishes, from North to South, East to West, on well-marked paths running through farmer's fields, woods, backyards, foothills and alps. In Italy it's common for two families to make a date for a Sunday afternoon to go walking together, with parents and children all taking part. Indeed, the secret to European health seems to be based on two quite simple practices: walking in sunlight and eating real food. I have followed this regime for decades and attribute to it what I have of health today.

IT WASN'T long after we moved to the country that I discovered a path in a secluded, neighboring park where I could illegally take Happy off leash to run reckless through the woods and terrorize the squirrels, an exercise that I believed to be highly therapeutic for both parties. The dog's benefits should be obvious but the squirrels', one could argue, are less so, as they appear to do an awful lot of rapid tree climbing and frantic branch leaping. But, how often do squirrels get to use such horrible language and with such passionate abandon? I like to think we are offering them a much-needed primal scream therapy to work off their frustrations with the limitations of an ever-diminishing natural kingdom. There are days when the truth of this loss depresses me so that I am tempted to join them in their tirades, but I can see no proof that it has improved the situation, so instead I walk along and thank the heavens for preserving this lovely little, light dappled corner of the forest for the handful of us who are able to enjoy it.

However beneficial this walk through the woods is for my animal companions, it is far more so for me. I would venture to say that this walk has enlightened me more than any other single activity. And, though I have days where I have not been able to quiet my busy mind entirely, I never leave completely disappointed.

This walk, which at an athletic pace can take forty-five minutes, has been stretched to at least twice this time by the amount of ooing and ahhing and pondering that goes on. In fact there are days when it threatens to go on the entire day, days when I am tempted to pull a "Walden" and move in. Some mornings the weather is so forbidding that my dogs (I usually have two going at a time these days) hesitate as I move out the door, as if I might have the good sense to reconsider, but they follow anyway because a dog can't stand to miss a squirrel. It is on just such a dreary day that I might be found deep in the wind-frantic woods, arrested by the birth of a sudden blissful speculation, while the dogs worry a pack of rain-drenched squirrels in a mad-rocking tree.

It is in the woods where I am sure of meeting with the teacher. Let me explain.

I LIKE to imagine that I have a true teacher, a figure much like the mythic Merlin, whose business it is to gently guide me toward the truth. My fantasy involves a mentor, master guide, compassionate being who walks beside me, neither of us seeming to set the pace, neither forcing nor slowing the speed, moving along at a mindful stroll and noticing things together. There are times when I point things out to the teacher and times when I sense the teacher directing my attention, as we move through what Dylan Thomas refers to in his "Poem In October" as "the parables of sunlight," the instruction of our days spent together on Planet Earth.

The teacher delights in pointing out examples of the easy harmony of the natural world. A flock of birds flying in unison (a phenomenon that has never been satisfactorily explained by science) is a favored sight. As this sight most often occurs while driving, the teacher and I can be quite a menace to motor safety as we weave along in jaw-dropping wonder while scores of birds, moving as one, lift, dart, alight, flawlessly in sync. We marvel, clapping and laughing like a couple of two-year-olds.

Animals offer wonderful examples of how to listen

to the teacher. When a domestic animal travels miles and miles alone across uncharted territory to find his owner, this is often tossed off as some sort of instinct, but I believe animals are simply much better able to listen to the teacher than we are. My friend Patty put it so simply when she suggested, "It's because they're so still." Stillness is a favorite theme of the teacher's, but its opposite, busyness, is something we worship in this country. We hear its devotees every day:

"How's it going?"

"Keeping busy."

"Good, good."

Our poor teachers! This is such a difficult atmosphere in which to conduct a lesson. Can you imagine if it were more like this?

"How's it going?"

"Finding stillness."

"Good, good."

The teacher loves to instruct through the behavior of animals and delights in sending me special sightings from the faunal kingdom. My head will suddenly wrench around, allowing me to catch some rare sight of owls at midday, groundhog picnics, wild turkey parades. Once, while driving down the road where I live, my head spun around to peer down a long driveway and there, as if to illustrate cross-species communication, was a cat and a deer in silhouette. The cat sat with nose lifted as the deer, with bended head, gently touched the nose of the cat with her own, in silent dialogue.

My head has craned and spotted all of my life. I once went on an African safari and managed to out-spot our Kenyan guide. I have, on several occasions, been rewarded with sightings in answer to specific requests. Once while driving home late one night with my husband, Matt, I said, "I don't believe I've ever seen a kestrel, have you? I would love to see a kestrel." The next morning, very early, Matt and I were awakened by a tapping on our second story bedroom window. We both sat up in bed to look at the source of the racket. A kestrel, a small bright-eyed hawk, perched just outside, pecked on the glass, stopped to stare at us, pecked some more, stared again, and flew away. I could almost feel the teacher's laughter shaking the bed. Of course, animal sightings must be simple wishes to grant. It's those others that are so tricky, the ones that require the tangle of human free will.

The teacher has an uncanny ability to find meaningful linkage among seemingly random occurrences. This talent is most pronounced when there is a time limit, say at a mingling party when one spends no more than fifteen minutes attempting to interact. If the person is new to me it seems inevitable that, within the first five minutes, we will uncover the one, often miniscule, thread that connects our lives. One or the other of us will mention some obscure fact from our past, brushing against a name or place when, like two electric wires crossing, we spark and flash, no longer strangers. I hope I am sufficiently grateful to the teacher when this occurs—it often feels quite miraculous.

"It's a small world," you often hear. But the teacher knows better than to draw such a banal conclusion. The world is vast, with billions of disparate lives. The magic of such specific connection among such fathomless possibilities is meant to awaken us to the miracle of unity and guidance. Or as Ralph Waldo Emerson suggests in "The Over-Soul," his own tribute to the teacher, "somewhat higher in each of us overlooks this by-play, and Jove nods to Jove from behind each of us."

I have felt the same sparkling connection and remarkable coincidence when meeting an animal. Indeed I felt it very strongly with my horse at our first meeting, and again, which I presume is much more rare, I felt it with the land on which she now lives.

Two

A FTER FIVE or so years of happy country living our beautiful, rural neighborhood faced a very real threat. Near our house is a hundred and some acre farm, which shares a border with the neighboring park where I walk in the morning.

The farm is mostly open grassland, a haven for ground-nesting birds, deer and fox, a feast of wildflowers and butterflies, and an important causeway for all the animals who live in the park and feed among the fields of our township. This farm was in danger of being sold to a developer whose plan would have totally altered the landscape of our surroundings: its peace, its natural beauty, its water supply, its sanctuary for the animals. We are a community of preservationists and offered to buy the farm collectively, but the owner wasn't interested in selling to a group.

One morning, sometime after our thwarted attempt to save the farm, while taking my daily walk through the forest of the park, I was sent perhaps the clearest message I have ever received from the teacher. I stood on the path, as if physically struck, and announced to my dogs, and surrounding trees, "We have to buy that farm." The thought was so pure, so filled with clear energy that I practically ran home to share the message with my husband. Having studied me carefully for many years, Matt responded without hesitation, "Let's make the call," and from that moment on he never wavered in his support of the idea.

The farm's history had been a dark one, with most owners buying in hopes of turning around and selling to developers as quickly as possible. The land, thankfully, was not septic-friendly and efforts to develop were always defeated. The recent threat involved a different type of sewage arrangement, which if approved, would not only have ruined our immediate neighborhood but would have had a domino effect that would completely change the canvas of our pastoral township.

The husband and wife who had bought the farm last were frustrated in their efforts to develop and finally frustrated with one another and ended up divorcing and dividing the farm. The wife landed on the hundred-acre portion consisting of mostly open fields, two large horse stables, some pastureland for grazing and a small house in which she would grow even more frustrated. Unable to sell, unable to make the horse operation viable, she slipped into despair and the farm began to show the signs of her depression. A previous owner had reportedly taken out insurance policies on his horses and picked them off one by one. In fact the place showed the signs of a long history of owners with negative intentions. It was mournfully unloved and the sadness was palpable. The current owner was so disconnected from the land that once, when I asked her about a very noticeable metal stake that stood in the middle of one of her back fields, she replied, "Puh, I never go back there." She prefaced most statements with a bitter out-breath. "Puh," she would say, "You can have the damned place. Puh, good luck."

Her bitterness permeated everything: house, barns, even pastures. It crept under my own skin very early into the negotiations, and if it hadn't been for Matt's faith in my initial inspiration, I never would have followed through with the purchase. As beautiful as the land was, it seemed to me shamefully disrespected and I doubted whether we could ever repair its dignity.

Somewhere during the negotiations I was introduced to a couple interested in running a farm and horse-boarding operation. They seemed very qualified and I was immediately comfortable with them. So comfortable that during this first meeting I said, "I'm

buying this farm to save it from development but,"—
and this was the phrase I was to repeat a hundred times
over the next year—"I don't intend to get involved."

If, as I believe, we existed in the heavens before we
came down into our lives, and if we have final words
before we leave that good place for this world, mine
must have been, "OK, I'll go down there, but don't ex-
pect me to get involved." This resistance to commit-
ting to life has been a plague to me, and for many years
I had longed to find a cure for my loose-handed grip on
the world. I am not speaking of the wise detachment
of the enlightened Buddhist, but of a certain tendency
to disengage when things didn't go as I wished them
to. Perhaps I lacked commitment and perseverance.
I sense the teacher's head bobbing up and down in
agreement.

WHEN WE closed on the farm we inherited a tenant
who rented one of the horse barns and took in a few
boarding horses. She had half a dozen beautiful Arabians, many in foal, which promised spring joy on the
farm. With the farmer's house now empty, she asked
to move in to be near her foaling mares, and she asked
that her mother might move in as well. There were two
apartments in the little house, making this a perfect
situation. How sweet, we thought, that she would wish
to live near her mother. We did think it a little odd that

she only dealt in cash and didn't have a phone number, a little odd that she had a different car every week. A little odd, perhaps, but this was rent and I didn't want to get involved.

The story that unfolded, after we had hired a private detective and been dragged through the Bucks County legal system, was a pattern of similar tales. This tenant would move into a rental situation, begin complaining, stop paying rent, rig up a bogus lawsuit to postpone eviction and buy herself months and months of free rent. Our predicament was further complicated by horses, which are rather difficult to evict (motels won't take them). Her lawsuit against us was easily thrown out of court. County court judges don't like to be bothered by such complaints as: Item number fifty-five: one riding crop discovered in field, having been run over by lawnmower.

As satisfying as it was to witness the justice system deliver, this justice was very slow in coming and the farm grew filthy, both spiritually and physically. I grew more and more disheartened. It was nearly impossible to think of anything but our difficult tenant and the destruction of any remnant of the farm's peace. By now the full-bodied confidence I had once had in my decision to buy the place had become anemic to the point of extinction. "Why?!" I would rail against the teacher, "Why did you tell me to buy that DAMNED FARM?! I told you I didn't want to get INVOLVED!!"

After several months, during which our tenant

(henceforward referred to as the "Evil Tenant") exhibited more and more psychotic facets of her personality, screaming and raging at us if we stepped foot onto the property, and as information poured in about past and present bad dealings, we received a phone call from a woman from Tennessee. She and her husband, wishing to retire from the horse business, had apparently shipped their beloved horses up to a woman in Bucks County, who claimed to have recently bought a farm with two horse barns and nice pastureland. The Tennessee couple was thrilled that their nine Arabians (many in foal) would be able to continue living together and on such a pretty farm. They had received a very small portion of the asked-for deposit but weren't immediately disturbed by this, as they were so pleased with the arrangement. The horses had been shipped up several months earlier and the driver given a tour of the farm by the Evil Tenant, complete with anecdotes of new farm ownership and horse doting. All seemed peachy until the check continued not to appear.

By the time the woman from Tennessee tracked Matt and me down she had spoken to the local police and the courthouse and had a reason for that queasy feeling that had been growing inside her. We assured her that as far as we knew our Evil Tenant had never paid a bill, hence the no checking account, the calls from the gas company and the electric company, the repossessed cars and the parade of constables delivering subpoenas to her door.

We planned a horse roundup.

Matt arranged the details. It was to take place on a Saturday morning. We knew the Evil Tenant's movements and were assured of her absence until noon. Matt's schedule was clear until midday as well. The couple from Tennessee planned to leave on the Friday morning before and spend the night about an hour away. The man who drove the large horse trailer was to meet Matt and me on the farm at ten o'clock in the morning, along with our farm managers, the couple from Tennessee and some guys from the local police. The plan went awry when the couple from Tennessee ate some questionable food on the road Friday and contracted a nasty case of food poisoning. They were naturally a bit sluggish Saturday morning, which meant a catastrophically late arrival, no Matt, and the possibility of the raging return of the Evil Tenant.

We had only rounded up a couple of the horses when she blew in, bringing hell with her. She ranted and raved and called the police. More police arrived to watch. She threatened me with all the venom in her tiny, shriveled heart and threw buckets and halters, anything she could find to distract the horses.

The entire local police community, the truck driver, the horse I was holding, and I watched as the farm managers and the poor dehydrated couple from Tennessee struggled to collect the other horses. One mare that had recently foaled was giving them trouble. She raced around the field, refusing all bribes and dodging all efforts to be caught, as the Evil Tenant waved her arms and screamed, hurling items at the pasture and the occasional choice phrase at me. After twenty minutes or so of this frustrating effort—there are few endeavors more frustrating than trying to catch a horse that doesn't wish to be caught— as I looked on, unable to be of any use, I decided to pray. Actually, it was more of a silent scream, directed at the teacher, that went something like "HELP! Help them catch that DAMNED HORSE, would you!!"

Soon after this the horse sighed and gave up, her foal trotting easily behind and into the trailer. The horse roundup was over.

But not so the reign of the Evil Tenant. That was to continue for another several months and I was involved—with every circling, despairing thought—entirely involved. After more visits to the courthouse, daily nonsense, and a new bogus suit against the poor couple from Tennessee, on the final day of the possibility of legal occupancy, the Evil Tenant moved. She moved, leaving the farm literally and figuratively black with filth.

A house that looked as if it had never seen a broom, wretched barns and horse stalls were nothing compared to the emotional defilement of the place. Ask anyone who lives in a recent war zone. It takes more than cleaning and rebuilding to heal this sort of contamination.

My neighbor Sue, who watched the horse trailers

and moving vans pull out in the Evil Tenant's caravan and drive down the road away from the farm, swears to have seen a snake moving along the road behind them, in slithering metaphor.

We had a bonfire to celebrate the recapture of the farm. In the barn we placed a black blob of material beneath a witch's hat to signify the melting away of the dark presence.

Slowly, very slowly, we took in one, then two, then three boarding horses. We gave the farmer's house a rest, adopted the sternest lease in town, and then carefully looked to fill it as well. The light was returning in ever increasing degrees and I started thinking once again about being less involved.

The spring after the reign of the Evil Tenant, a white fawn was born on the property. Matt and I would walk the summer sunlit fields in order to spot her. Rarely disappointed, we took it as a positive sign for the farm.

Apart from these visits, I began to disengage.

Three

MY FIRST encounter with farm living occurred at the age of nine when my newly divorced mother moved the family onto our grandparents' gentleman's farm in Louisville, Kentucky, taking over the house that my grandparents had built when my mother was a child. There was a farmer who cared for the farm while we lived there, hired by my late grandfather. His name was Mr. Wilson and he lived on the property. Soon after we moved, my mother asked Mr. Wilson whether he would look for some old farm horses for the children. Many years later my mother admitted to being terrified that one of us might be injured by this rash move on her part, but her desire to offer us joy during the chaotic years after the divorce won out over her fears.

One day three horses arrived, well-seasoned, you might call them: calm, miles and miles out of shape, finely aged like bourbon in a barrel, and come to think of it, shaped rather like barrels. We gave them names, although I am sure they had been given such things before, perhaps several times over. But my sister Janey and my brother Robin and I gave them the names Molly, Dolly and Prince. Molly was the youngest of the three, a full-figured bay, and when Mr. Wilson saw her he said to the man who was selling her, "That mare is in foal." This is an old trick of the trade for selling horses. If you sell a mare when she is pregnant, you can be assured that her hormones are ironed out and she will come across as respectfully docile.

The horse trader roundly denied the accusation.

"If she has a foal," the man countered, "I'll come back for more money."

Janey and Robin and I learned to saddle up the horses and ride around the farm on them. We were thrown off, rubbed off and occasionally just slid off for no good reason. My mother's fears were played out daily, but somehow we always managed to bounce. Every spill was a cause of much entertainment, so that we almost looked forward to falling off, or better yet, witnessing a sibling's fall. The scene would have us in stitches for days.

As well as taking care of the horses, Mr. Wilson oversaw a herd of Black Angus beef cattle on the farm, and he would occasionally allow the three of us to round up and attempt to move the cows from one field to another. These were mamas and babies, about fifty in number, and for the most part, perfectly reasonable animals.

We three would climb up on our horses and systematically move in an ever-tightening circle around the herd, endeavoring to force the animals through the gate. This process was simple enough until one of the calves would escape from the circle and run around behind the horses. While the rest of the herd filed placidly through the open gate and into the new field, and after the three of us had congratulated ourselves on our cowboy skills, the calf behind us would let out a small mournful cry and one of the mamas would lift her head. After three and a half seconds the calf's mama and all forty-eight of her friends would barrel back through the gate, in stampede fashion, to recover the lost child, causing our horses to make a mad dash for the far reaches of the farm and refuse to have anything to do with cows the rest of the day.

Mr. Wilson would look on, bemused, and then whistle for his sheepdog, Tuffy. "Go get 'em, Tuffy," he'd say, and in seconds the dog would have successfully herded the entire crew back through the gate and into the new field.

Again and again, when the horses grew more trusting and the cows needed to be moved to better grazing, we would saddle up for another attempt at cattle-wrestling, with the same results.

However frustrating to the novice cow-wrangler, the willingness of the herd to leave a fresh new pasture of rich grazing to retrieve the one missing child was lovely to witness. Yes, cows are herd animals, and this could be chalked up as instinct, but still, I find it a precious metaphor. I suspect that humans might be herd animals as well, or perhaps there is a little spark of the herd instinct in each of us.

This is a slightly different metaphor than the one of the good shepherd, always prepared to return for the one lost sheep. Perhaps it is more like followers of the Buddha and their willingness to take the Bodhisattva vow: to postpone personal nirvana until all sentient beings are free. I think of all the people whom I have met who might spend their days in contented enlightenment, but instead choose to serve humanity. I have known several who would pass up rich pastures to help a lost soul, like my friend Steve Werlin whose book *To Fool The Rain* outlines his work with the ultra-poor of rural Haiti. His job for the micro-finance organization FONKOZE, requires days of off-road hiking in order to serve his clients, all women and children who have been identified as catastrophically poor. One catastrophe—an illness, hurricane, injury—could quickly cause the whole family to starve. For a year and a half,

Steve will visit these families weekly to give them the tools to lift themselves out of poverty. Someday, perhaps six hundred years from now, I will have the courage to take on such a job.

AFTER HALF a year or so, I grew bored of the saddle and tossed it out to ride around bareback, and Janey and Robin grew bored with horses altogether.

In the meantime, Molly's belly grew larger and larger and she finally gave birth to a pretty little bay filly. Sadly, after just a few weeks, the filly was diagnosed with cancer. She developed a tumor on her face and one on her leg. One day I overheard my mother saying, "She has to be put down, but the vet wants to wait a bit and allow Margaret to get used to the idea."

I went to my room and brooded. I was ten at the time and remember thinking how very odd adults must be to be willing to cause a beautiful creature such as this one to suffer more than she need suffer to postpone my sorrow. I didn't want the little filly to have a moment's pain. I hope I prayed for her, because I don't remember talking to the grownups. I assumed that they must know better what to do. A day later the filly's leg broke from the tumor and the vet hastily put her down.

Perhaps this experience has something to do with my ease around the subject of euthanasia for animals, but I more suspect that my attitude has to do with my belief that every spirit lives on. This and the understanding that where there is love involved, with a human or a beloved animal, there is the possibility of ultimate reunion.

I mourned the little filly—of course I did—and have mourned hundreds of animal passings since that day. I have mourned dead animals on the side of the road. I have sat with dying birds and prayed for their release. I recently discovered a dying sea turtle in the middle of a little bay while kayaking in the Bahamas. I gave him a name—I do that now for animals that look as if they are soon to depart the world. I have an intuition that this might be useful to them in the world to come. I told the turtle that he need not postpone his passing one minute more. I placed my hand on his back and begged for his release. I returned an hour later to find that he had died.

I find animals to be quite simple to mourn. Simple, I say, not easy. There is rarely the attendant complication of difficult relationships, as is the case with humans. One can simply be sad.

I was sad for the filly, sad for the filly's mother, but I would not have wished for the little animal to have a moment more of suffering before her release. We gave Molly a period of rest and then I began to ride again, asking friends to join me.

My friend Boo often rode with me and would always choose Prince to be her not-so-princely steed. Prince was the biggest barrel of them all, a chestnut mutt with a sneaky sense of humor. He spent his time with Boo thinking of ways to mess with her. If she approached him with a bridle, he would suddenly look off into the distance, as if there was something terrifically fascinating out there. Boo would inevitably postpone putting the bit in his mouth and turn to have a look, at which point Prince would swing his head around and bite her. She always fell for this trick. One time he tried the head-in-the-distance number on her, but instead of biting her, he lifted his big hoof and brought it down on her foot. Boo was a great satisfaction to Prince because she was so dramatic. "Aaaack!" she would scream, while Prince looked off in the distance, unfazed. He knew this was just a warm up to their rides together and seemed to be quietly plotting how he was going to unseat her. He had a varied repertoire of ways to do this: some well-worn ones, such as scraping along fence posts, aiming for low-hanging branches, or trotting along and suddenly stopping altogether, causing Boo a forward pitch over the neck. If none of these tactics worked, he would start bucking. In fact, he never broke into a canter without trying to buck Boo off.

After many pitches and re-mountings, Boo developed the grabbing-est legs in Kentucky. We could have entered her in a rodeo. Indeed we both learned to stick to our horses like warts, clinging on as we dashed around higgledy-piggledy, jumping, herding, goofing around. The horses rarely surprised us, but on occasion would manage to pop us off their backs.

You can never entirely trust a horse. I learned this when I was nine, and was to revisit the fact in my mid-forties with the arrival of Allie.

Four

THE SUMMER after the Evil Tenant departed, Allie arrived on the farm. She was six years old at the time and fresh off the racetrack. Her owner and small-time trainer placed her with us while he underwent heart surgery. The moment I saw her I knew she would be mine. "That's the prettiest horse I've ever seen," I said. "Her owner isn't going to make it back to training and she's going to be mine." As strongly as I felt this to be true, as much as I understood this to be a sort of heads up from the teacher, the premonition was attended by an immediate swarm of doubt-mosquitoes. "A horse? You're going to take on a horse? Isn't the farm enough? Horses are rather … involving!"

When Allie arrived on our farm, she wore a halter, which must have belonged to one of the owner's previous horses. It read "Margaret's Nora D." Even her halter spoke of my possession. As clear as this was, I was madly resistant. I can hear the teacher chuckling.

I had entirely reasoned myself out of any thought of horse possession by the time I learned that my prediction had come true. Allie's owner, deciding to retire from the training business, gave her to us for the board he owed, and she was mine, or the farm's, as I preferred to look at it.

One of the not-so-endearing stories that attended Allie was that she had recently spooked and taken a jockey on an unplanned joy ride. I hadn't had a horse since I was sixteen and now I was forty-six. Surely I was not the intended owner for this horse. I ducked and hid from her. I avoided the barn where she lived and tried not to notice her in the fields. Allie began to lose muscle tone, (not a hardship as she was a bit muscle-bound), and memory of the track (a very good thing). One of the women at the barn began to ride her a little. "Perfect," I said to myself, "she may have her."

One day I was talking to our farm manager's youngest child Halee, who was five years old at the time and a wise old soul. I told her that when I was her age I announced that when I grew up I was going to live on a farm and sleep in a barn full of animals. She looked at

its dense foliage plunging me in the shade of apathy. I grew weak, breakable.

It wasn't that I didn't have fun, that I didn't enjoy and love, but behind every reminder of man's inhumanity was the dreary refrain: "Oh well, maybe I'll be allowed to leave the world soon."

There were days in my twenties when this thought haunted my every hour. I was not suicidal. I had no impulse to expedite this plan. I simply allowed that I would welcome the opportunity to go back to my creator, to my home, at any time. My bags were packed, so to speak. I never spoke to a professional about this looping, dismal refrain, and have only confessed it to a handful of people.

In retrospect, I am grateful that I didn't try and "find a cure" for this condition, because there were two sides to these thoughts: one dark and leading nowhere, and the other filled with sunlight, with the promise of awakening.

The dark was obvious, the sense of not belonging, of hoping to be released from the duties of living. The light was grand. It began in me the search for deeper meaning, the curiosity to uncover the world behind the physical. This drew me to a lifetime of reading, and searching out those who professed to have had glimpses, visions, ecstatic encounters, mystical experiences. It drew me to the books of the great religions and lasting philosophies, it opened me to the thoughts of the great teachers of all faiths. It led me to the writings of those who had, against all obstacles, been able to move beyond the constraints of the popular philosophy of their times, and to search for the foundation of truth.

This quest led me to the writings of the great, free-thinking, transcendent writers. It was this hunger that prompted me to discover the writings of George MacDonald, Ralph Waldo Emerson, Emanuel Swedenborg, Julian of Norwich, Epictetus, Marcus Aurelius, Hafiz: all rebellious voices, fighting against the narrowness of popular religious thinking during their times. These writers have been my constant companions, lifting me up to view the world from a place where I am able to embrace its paradoxes.

The effort to find the meaning beyond what the world appears to present has been the greatest work of my life. I value this curiosity and its answered treasures more than any of the gifts I have been given along the way. There is no doubt of this left in me.

I met a woman once who professed to be a kindred, sensitive spirit, especially around the treatment of animals. We lamented together the history of abuse of our brothers and sisters in the animal kingdom. She went on to say that she did not feel as if she belonged in a world where animals were killed for entertainment. She said things like, "We aren't like those people. We don't belong." She seemed to wish to make a club out of us, and our sensitivities, a club of two. I wanted to help her, but couldn't think what to say. In retrospect I should have warned, "Oh but you must be very careful not to stay there! Don't get stuck at the point of sensitivity and refuse to participate. The only way to a better place, a kinder place, is through this world, not around it. Please don't hold your breath hoping to be released."

I wanted to tell her about my struggles around this sense of belonging. That if my life on this earth were a transatlantic cruise, there have certainly been times when I suspected the teacher might have booked me passage on the wrong ship.

I've spent far too much of life questioning whether I belonged here, whether some grand mistake may have been made, and I was really meant to incarnate on quite a different planet. Perhaps, I muse, the teacher and I might have located a kinder vessel, where war, slavery, and the grotesque abuses of women, children and animals couldn't exist.

I wanted to tell this woman that there have been plenty of moments when I have cried, "Let me off this damned thing!"—I see the teacher's arms rise up in exasperation—when I have ranted and threatened to leave the planet. I'm ashamed to say how many times this wish for escape was my first response when faced with atrocity.

I WISH I could come up with a snappy answer for those kindred spirits that wrestle, as I do, with the desire for an escape route. It is a condition that must be treated with great care. One cannot school these sensitive ones, as the teacher knows. In fact the teacher allows me to make all sorts of unnerving mistakes without the delivery of a single sermon. These are like fantastic pratfalls into large ruts of pointless thinking. As with my repetitive desire to leave the planet, the teacher will watch, wait, assured that someday I will begin to see the absurdity of my thinking. It is the teacher's difficult job to get me to cry for, and then laugh at myself. I'm afraid it is my only hope. Oh, but I cringe at the thought of how many hours of boring inner monologue the teacher must suffer before I am able to shift my thinking.

I imagine there are times when the good teacher is keenly bored with me. I can only hope that there are others, friends, to lighten the load.

When my thoughts are circling around some tiresome subject, one that I have stomped around perhaps two million times—"Why was I born?" could be used as a general example—I can almost imagine a captive, heavenly audience watching my life as if it were a film. I see them sitting attentively in their cinema seats, wings tucked carefully at their sides, as a question appears in my mind: "Why the heck was I put down here?"

One of them rolls his eyes.

"Am I expected to do something with this life?"

I hear another groan. "Uuuhhh"

"Is there some sort of plan, something specific you'd like me to accomplish?"

The teacher stands and stretches, gives the others a look, "Any of you guys want some popcorn?"

If there is a process of atonement or curative retribution after this life, it may be to sit through endless hours of one's own repetitive questioning, like watching the tedious footage (dailies, I believe they are called in the film business) of the same circling doubts. The idea chills me.

I HAVE found that questions around the purpose of my incarnation during this era, through this family, in this country, on this beautiful and ailing planet are most easily answered by looking for the places where I belong.

Six

I BELONGED IN my family. I understand there are many who don't feel this way, who never sensed that they fit with the people with whom they spent their early years. I'm fortunate to have felt that I was meant to live among the members of my tribe. Their beneficial influence has been central and lasting, and this early sense of belonging has allowed me to weather the storms of later isolation.

I am sure, for instance, that I was meant to be my grandmother's grandchild, for she had a most precious effect on me. Her name was Jane and, for as long as I knew her, she was an anthroposophist. For those of you who have never heard of such a thing, it is a person who follows the teachings of the pragmatic Austrian mystic Rudolf Steiner, who wrote and philosophized on just about every subject imaginable.

Jane's mystical view of the world was barrels more life shaping than any amount of time spent in our local Episcopal church in the outskirts of Louisville, Kentucky. Other than my time spent in the choir, which held moments of transcendence, I'm not aware of the faintest spiritual influence from my weekly visits to this church. Since this time, I have found a handful of profoundly gifted ministers and don't wish to disparage the church or the office of the priesthood. I merely refer to my first introduction to the institution.

My grandmother's child-friendly interpretation of some of the thoughts of Rudolf Steiner had an exquisitely enlivening influence on me as I began to comprehend the world. When I looked at a growing thing—a tree, for instance—I was given to understand that not only was this a physical, but also a spiritual being and therefore vital to the order of the universe. Indeed, there were those in the spirit world whose job it was to nurture these beings and it was possible to contact them on behalf of their charges. Even stones had such spirit selves and corresponding aid. I understood that there was a tremendous amount of activity going on about me that was invisible to my physical senses.

I was told that my love connected me to the nurturing spirits of all life, and that if I dearly loved a tree, for instance, I could possibly affect the health of that tree, could ask for its protection while its spirit receded in the winter, that it might come back with greater strength in the spring.

And, if each stone, each plant had beings in the spirit world to look after it, how much more was I watched over—not because I was more entitled—but because I was more complex, with many levels other than my physical one. The concept of this divine and very intimate concern for my soul, the idea of the teacher, was just beginning to take shape in me.

I understood that love, particularly love expressed through prayer, was a tremendous force, palpable, altering, that our prayers were listened to by God and a host of angels, and that this aid was always there for us. In my darkest, most despairing hours, I have never believed that I was alone.

I have often wondered, who, what, where would I be without this introduction to the world. Even with this early instruction, it has taken me fifty years to trust this world of spirit aid so entirely that I can honestly say that I do not live in a world of random occurrences, chance encounters, or isolation. I do not live in the world in which I believe many people live. I live in a world where the spirit in all life is transcendent and matter cannot matter without it, and where the growth of that ever-rising spirit is the central reason for our presence here. I live in a world where the progress of my own small spirit may be as important as the progress of the human spirit in its entirety, essential to the ordering of the universe, and therefore closely watched and guided.

I live in a world where my curious spirit is always being fed, carefully and painstakingly. I live in a world where even the smallest encounter with the divine is important, if only to teach us to listen. I live in a world where a trip to the grocery store might allow a message to slip through, where, if I find myself mystifyingly stalled in an aisle, staring at a bottle of mayonnaise, I might engage in a lively discussion with the teacher. "Why are you making me look at that jar of mayonnaise when I *know* there is a full jar at home?" Stare, stare… "I know what you're trying to tell me, but I think you are wrong," I continue my inner dialogue, and continue to stare. Depending on which way I go, I either find myself one day, out of mayonnaise and cursing myself, or thanking the teacher profusely for saving the day, with a pile of fresh bread and turkey and a house full of guests.

The modern mystic Lorna Byrne, who writes about the angelic kingdom, suggests that it is in these very small moments that we learn to listen, that essentially the grocery store is a training ground. Eventually these moments will lead to our learning to listen for more and more important information, such as where we might be of use to the world, who we might wish to befriend, or which books we should read.

ALTHOUGH IT has been over thirty years since we were introduced by the teacher, I can remember the moment I met Ralph Waldo Emerson as if it were captured on film. I sat in my brother's house, resting in the gentle, rolling green fields of Kentucky with a handful of like-minded souls, as we discussed thoughts, both written and spoken, which had broken through the mundane to lift and enlighten us.

"I have a quote I'd like to share with you," announced a friend, as he pulled out a hefty hardbound volume. I couldn't make out the title on its binding.

He began to read.

> *"How dear, how soothing to man, arises the idea of God, peopling the lonely place, effacing the scars of our mistakes and disappointments! When we have broken our god of tradition, and ceased from our god of rhetoric, then may God fire the heart with his presence... He has not the conviction, but the sight, that the best is the true... He is sure that his welfare is dear*

> *to the heart of being... He believes that he
> cannot escape from his good."*

Had I been introduced to this voice at too young an age, I know I would have avoided him the rest of my life. As it was I will never forget that day.

"Who is that?" I asked, eager, awake.

"Emerson," was the answer.

Little bells began to ring in my head. The stars came out.

"And is anyone allowed to walk into a bookstore and purchase this man's writings?" I asked, "I mean, you don't have to belong to some secret society?"

"Anyone." I was assured.

"Thank you dear," I whispered to the unseen, "You are too good to me."

BOOK RECOMMENDATIONS are among the top required skills of the teacher, and I always marvel at the accuracy of content and timing. I'm not alone in being so well targeted. My friend Sarah has a communal laundry room in her Manhattan apartment building that acts as a sort of pass-it-along library. When the tenants finish a book that might interest someone else, they stick it on a shelf in the laundry room. Whenever Sarah describes a book she has discovered, often out of print, touting its significance to her own journey,

has led me: the heart of my husband, home, friends, siblings, dogs, books. If none of these are within my line of vision, I fall back on the horizon, or my sense of belonging to that world of which my grandmother Jane spoke, with all of its loving guidance.

When I am witness to some man-made abomination, such as my country's constant involvement in wars, or the accelerated destruction of this dear planet, I crawl out on the deck of this strange ship of a world on which I ride and look at the horizon, taking in the uncontaminated air of this larger existence. It is here where I find hope, possibility of change, broader vision. My lungs fill with fresh vigor. I feel the teacher next to me.

"Surely there must be a reason," I sigh, "some purpose for this particular passage on this particular vessel, at this particular time in history."

I sense the teacher smiling.

"Surely, if there is a way that I can be of service to its direction, this will be revealed."

I can almost hear the letting go of a long-held breath.

"In the meantime, its course being too grand and complex for me to comprehend," I continue, "perhaps it's best to trust the navigation to some steadier hand than my own."

Seven

SEVERAL MONTHS before Allie's injury I took on my third dog, a puppy named Cotton. Having three dogs, two of which were at opposite ends of life, with one in need of massive amounts of exercise, and the other very near transition to the next world, I was able to visit the barn far less frequently. I reasoned with myself that I would return to Allie when the weather grew cooler, and my puppy more civilized.

In the meantime, I was spending more and more time in the woods.

The deep forest remained the place where I felt most inclined to worship, my surest point of connection with the divine.

It was in the woods ... tell th[e] ... who it was I loved ... why. This was ... place where I could ... for those whom I was currently unable to ... promise to try to find creative ways of doing ... the future. It was along my walk that I could ... try to be more like those who were easy to ... like my dogs. Mundane thoughts would bounce around the trees like pinballs. Grocery lists and bodily complaints made a terrible racket. The petty seemed to have no place in the woods. I do not wish to imply that all of my thinking was of a positive nature. The woods had, in fact, been privy to some of my deepest doubts and sorrows. They would listen, like a great silent mother, and send me back into the world with an encouraging pat on the back.

After many years of daily devotion along my walk in the woods, I began to wonder whether I should supplement this practice with a periodic visit to a church. I do love the warmth of community and its power for compassionate action. And the occasional rousing sermon has been known to bring me gratefully to my knees. I had heard of a minister in the area who liked to toss in a smattering of Buddhist thought with his Christian advice. I thought that perhaps I would make a Sunday sojourn to his church of ... (I can't recall the protestant denomination).

The morning was gorgeous, and I had cut my walk short in order to dash over to and into the preacher's rather airless church. The sermon was fine, and in-

awkward with the call and response, uneasy with the minister speaking for the children, it wasn't enough to suffer a sudden attack of sleep-sickness, but the sign must be so fantastic, so preposterous—a W.A.S.P., for goodness sakes— to force me to stop and listen. "Gawlee," I languidly reasoned, "perhaps I don't belong here."

When I systematically ignore all preliminary signs from the teacher, the messages designed for me grow more and more obvious, absurdly so. They multiply and appear around every corner. And, if I willfully march down a road that is leading me away from my truth, the small signs will grow to the size of billboards, always with the same message: "This choice does not give you life. Now do you understand?"

"I do," I answer, grateful for the teacher's steady perseverance. "Thank you."

I returned to my woods.

Eight

A FTER SEVERAL years of early morning walking, my path through the woods introduced me to a man I will call Barry. Or was it the teacher who brought us together? Barry was unlike anyone I had ever met. A child spirit in an adult body, Barry could not drive, and rarely handled money, but managed to somehow charm his way through life with his peculiarities and willingness to be useful. He frequently walked my path and we would often encounter one another.

Barry's body at the time was somewhere in the neighborhood of seventy years old, wiry, overused. If Barry were an insect, he would be an ant in beetle's clothing. His belt was the only item that came anywhere near his flesh—the rest dangling loosely from an overly cinched middle. His teeth appeared to have been designed for a man much larger than himself as well, causing his mouth to rattle noisily when he spoke—an activity that Barry indulged in almost constantly. He proudly boasted of a Native American heritage (a dubious claim) and advertised the notion by a network of feathers and beads that hung from his neck.

Like Charles Dickens, he walked over twenty miles a day, but without the same level of literary productivity, though I imagine that he had as many bouncing words in his head.

I was made aware of Barry's approach well before I spotted him by the lively conversation he was having with himself, the only person, I might add, who could comfortably understand him. Barry's mystifying manner of speech caused most people to listen with slack-jawed incomprehension.

I managed, after many years of morning meetings, to speak at least enough "Barry" to get by. In fact I was often called upon to translate for the other early morning visitors to this patch of woods, of which there were only two: my friends Pam and Wink, both dog owners and, like myself, stubbornly unwilling to recognize a day too lousy for a walk.

"Good morning!" we would sing out to one another. "Beautiful day!" we'd chirp, as the wind whipped, sleet cut though bitter, single digit temperatures. We liked to stop and chat on the worst of mornings as if it were a balmy day in June. "And they said it was going to be bad today!" we'd share with incredulity. "Just look at it!" we'd offer, glancing around serenely, as dogs shivered, trees groaned, ice choked our nostrils. It was often at these meetings that Barry would come along the path, nose like an open faucet, teeth rattling, feathers drooping, the only one willing to admit that the morning was not the finest the area had seen in some time. "Fgtmagdmuckbts" he'd mutter.

"Oh, you forgot your muck boots?" I'd sing out for my friends.

"Stn bythu G'dm der." He'd answer.

"Left them sitting by the door?" I'd enunciate, avoiding the description.

"Goddamn" was Barry's favorite adjective. Once he told me that he had been offered some wine one night, of which he said, "namykinwn."

"Not your kind of wine?" I repeated, "What kind of wine is your kind of wine?" I inquired.

"Rhd"

"Ah," I continued, "and what kind of wine was it you were offered?"

"Eddybee."

"Oh, I've heard of elderberry wine. Interesting," I answered.

"Yeh," he continued, and I translate. "They take the goddamn elderberry and they smash the goddamn things, make wine."

"Hm, I see. And where was this?"

"Seen-Sit-Sen."

"Ahah." I had been hearing about this place for several years. It was high-up in the baffling Barry lexicon, always delivered with sharp percussion. Seen! Sit! Sen! Sometimes the last syllable was eliminated altogether, (Seen! Sit!), making it even more enigmatic. It wasn't until I deduced that every mention of the "Seen Sit Sen" was connected to some form of partying fun, and that busses were often leaving this mysterious place, delivering Barry to even more fun, picnic kind of fun, that I figured it out. Ahah! I lit up, "the Senior Citizens Center!"

The Senior Citizen's Center was the place that Barry frequented, or some might say cruised, for "wmn." He anticipated his outings with the senior citizens with almost the same degree of excitement that preceded his birthday every year.

"Just three more days," Barry would announce.

"Three more days until what?" I'd ask.

"My Birthday!" he would answer, as if it were Election Day and I hadn't bothered to follow the news.

During those years Barry walked most days to a small village on the Delaware River, just three miles from where we met in the mornings. I am not entirely certain why, but I was told (by Barry) that whatever service he rendered there was of profound use to those to whom it was offered. Most of Barry's tales were of being indispensably beneficial to someone needing help that only he, Barry could provide: help clearing a driveway, help burying a dead horse, help understanding a quirky animal. Most of us, according to Barry, would have been quite lost without him. I, for instance, would never have been able to manage to load my three dogs back into the car at the end of my walk without Barry there to direct them.

"Git up there! You get on up there in the G'dm car."

You see, very helpful.

Barry was full to spilling with such stories of service, like the one about the old man who needed Barry to help him with his horse. I'm not clear on the history, but Barry had apparently become so indispensable that the old man asked Barry to care for his horse if anything happened to him. One morning, according to Barry, the horse broke out of his pasture, and trotted over to Barry's house (a considerable trot) to find him.

I translate:

"Woke up, G'dm horse head's in my G'dm winda."

"What did you do?" I asked.

"I said, what's wrong? Old man dead??" He paused dramatically, and continued. "Jumped on his back, rode up there, old man's dead. Piece of paper on the floor next to him. Give the horse to Barry."

Barry often carried a pair of old field glasses and claimed to know where a nesting pair of eagles was hidden deep in the park. He reported on their habits, the progress of their offspring. He worried that they might be disturbed by visitors to the park.

One Thanksgiving morning I met Barry on the path along the canyon in the park. We stood discussing what might be going on at the Seen Sit Sen on that grateful day when we heard an unfamiliar cry above our heads. It was a whispery quiet morning and the strange call pierced the silence. We looked up to discover a battalion of huge white birds, their wing tips dipped in black. "What are those?" I asked, in wonder.

"No-Gee."

"Snow geese, beautiful."

Barry knew his animals. Many of his anecdotes attested to a strong kinship with the world of fauna—although his finesse with my dogs was all but imperceptible. The only reaction Barry elicited from them seemed to be disappointment over the absence of anything edible in his pockets. Yet I always assumed that he enjoyed a sort of power to enter their world. Many of his narratives, although a tad outlandish, might have been viewed as reasonable in Barry-land. Once I asked him how exactly he managed to penetrate an animal's mind. "Do you send them mental images, assuming, as some suggest, that animals communicate in pictures?" I posed.

Barry looked at me as if I'd just landed from another planet. "No, I just talk to them!"

Silly me!

My faith in Barry's kinship with the beasts might excuse the fact that I did not view the griffin sighting as immediately preposterous. It came up while he was talking about the "G'dm rangr," (the park ranger, whom Barry viewed with the deepest distrust). My suspicion was that the ranger did not speak, nor had ever bothered to learn, one word of "Barry." I couldn't exactly understand what the two had been discussing but Barry grew quite animated and repeated, "Don't worry about that, worry about that G'dm cat!"

"Cat?" I replied.

"Sum'bitch could hurt someone!"

Oh yes, I forgot to mention that most animals, no matter how much loved, are characterized as "sum'bitches" Not sure why. In fact, Barry told me one day, "You shave a G'dm Rhodesian Ridgeback, sum'bitch'll fall flat dead." I cannot speak for the truth of this statement, but surely Barry would not wish this particular fate on the son-of-a-bitch.

On further questioning about the cat, Barry described an animal that he had seen in the park that was, if my memory serves, larger than a Labrador, with jet-black, long wavy hair, ears like a cat and the leaping talents of a man-sized cricket.

He'd spotted the "sum'bitch" several times and the "G'dm rangr" wouldn't get out of his "G'dm car" to look for the "G'dm thing."

In discussing the sighting with my husband, I could tell that he, like the "G'dm rangr," was chalking this beast up to mythology. I felt the need to defend. "But I really don't think that Barry would fabricate a sighting like this. In fact most of his stories are quite painfully mundane." Like the one about the fan-belt-thingy that broke on the snow-removal-contraption. It's during such sagas that I will say, "Barry, is there an end to this story, because I have a life to live." He laughs and plows forward, stretching the account to even greater dramatic lengths, about the flabbed-out belt-thingy on the G'dm truck. Or the sum'bitch that's lying in his stall, barely breathing. At some point in these stories, the desperate owners of said busted machine or un-well animal have to call in Barry, who swoops in like a super-medicine-man-hero, to fix the G'dm sum'bitch.

But I digress, and will return to my discussion with my husband. "There are misguided people in this world," I suggested, "who buy exotic animals and then release them in parks when they grow unmanageable. This creature could be one of these." I held by this argument for several days, until I saw Barry again.

"Seen anything unusual lately?" I inquired.

"Nope," he answered.

"Nothing? No animals, no strange sightings?" I probed.

"Hmm," he thought for a moment" "saw a track, paw print, big. Sum'bitch was this big." He held his hands far enough apart to comfortably hold a water-melon. "Yep. Seen it before."

"What do you think it is? I asked

"Sasquatch." he answered without hesitation.

"I see," I replied, and went home with my tail between my legs to confess the conversation to my husband.

Once Barry crossed the credibility line, he seemed to take flight. The next morning he told me a story about being sucked through a snow blowing machine and coming out the other end like a "dishrag." Perhaps this is why he was so often called upon to fix those machines, being so familiar with their insides. Apparently he was taken to the hospital in his dishrag state and the doctor attending pronounced him dead, and "put him in another room." After some time, a "Man from Washington DC" walked by the dishrag that was Barry and thought he saw some life. This "Man from DC" then proceeded to open up Barry's entire body from the toes up through leg bones, thigh bones, rib cage, shoulder bones, up to the head, to discover nothing but rubble. At which point, the remarkable "Man from Washington DC" methodically replaced every bone in Barry's body with steel. Apparently it was this metal skeleton that had raised Barry to the mega-mega-super-medicine-man-hero level—well, this and his super-willingness to help.

Barry had an Achilles' heel within this steel bone structure, and that was that he wanted a woman more than anything in the world. To be more exact, Barry wanted a wife. The idea of there being a match for such an original defied all reason, although if perseverance had any power, a match would certainly be found. The initial question he posed to every woman he met was, "You married?" He skipped all preliminaries and cut right to the chase. If the answer was yes, he would huff, laugh and move on instantly.

"That other one, the one with the two little dogs, she married?" he would continue.

"Yes, I'm afraid she is."

"Hm. Huff." He'd pause for less than a second. "That one I seen out on the road on the horse, she married?"

I hesitated to wonder whether I might be allowed a small, well-meaning lie. "I can't exactly say, but she very well might be."

Barry was never quite satisfied with any one of the three women who walked the path in the woods.

"Where's that other one, the one comes here with the black and white dog?"

"What am I, pickled beets?" I was often tempted to ask. "I haven't seen her today."

"She married?"

The tricky part to taking Barry seriously was that he was so comical. Once, when he was telling me something about which he felt strongly, (perhaps it was the G'dm rangr) he stopped, leaned over, slapped his leg, and exploded with laughter.

"What is it?" I asked. "Did I miss something?" I had been having a rather difficult time comprehending "Barry-ish" that day.

He wheezed and straightened up. "Forgot my teeth!"

Barry told me of dozens of "wmn" who had been under consideration for matrimony. He would describe them with little subtlety: "She's kinda on the heavy side but she's ok." I always assumed that the objects of his amorous attention were entirely unaware of the honor he wished to bestow on them, that most were minor characters in his life, seen briefly on the road, met awkwardly at a picnic.

One early Christmas morning, after a face-numbing, finger-aching, wind-whipped walk, I spotted Barry. I had just managed to pile the dogs back in the car and was heading out of the parking lot when I stopped to wish him a merry Christmas. Some mornings, I must confess, I would nip away swiftly, if I could do so without offense, in fear of being waylaid by another endlessly long Native American super-hero legend, while hungry, whining dogs fussed in the back of my car. But it was Christmas, for goodness sakes.

"Merry Christmas, Barry, how are you?" I asked, rolling down my window.

Barry said nothing, but pointed to his eyes. I could see that they were damp, presumably from the weather, which I could readily acknowledge now that I was heading home.

"Oh I know, the wind is a terror today, isn't it?" I offered.

"Nope," Barry answered. "Tears."

"You've been crying?" I replied. "Why?

"Don't have a wife."

"Oh, I'm so sorry," I gasped. I was so sorry. Sorry that I had ever made light of his sad, sad unanswered desire. I felt terrible.

"Life can be so disappointing," I offered.

"Yep... well, you gotta keep going."

Poor Barry. I cringed to think that I had viewed his hopes of finding a wife as the adolescent craving of a muddled mind.

"I hope your dreams come true."

I HAVE come to suspect that where there is that much depth of feeling, of unsatisfied longing, there will come, at some point along the great eternal path, an answer of equal profundity. Of course Barry has a whole, fully realized spirit somewhere, even though only a fraction was presented to us here. At some point, perhaps in the far, far future, I imagine that Barry will have his honorable longing answered. He will meet that wife of his one day, maybe two hundred years from now, both of them comfortably clothed in their eternal souls.

I can see Barry waking up one morning, after years and years of wedded joy, turning to his wife and saying, "Oh, I was just having the kookiest dream. I was searching and searching for you, but I couldn't find you. I was in the deep woods and there were dogs everywhere, big yellow dogs, little brown dogs, black and white dogs. There were three women in the dream too. They were the strangest of all, wandering around in the most awful weather, as if it were midsummer. I could never keep them straight in my mind, which were married, which weren't. I just knew that none of them was you. I woke up crying... Thank God it was only a dream."

Nine

U P TO the point of Allie's injury I would describe myself as a "fair-weather horse owner," preferring to ride when the footing was good and my schedule allowed. I was a "horse owner," not a "horse person." The latter category, in my opinion, comprises those who visit their animals every day and border dangerously on the obsessive; the type that nail copious notes to their horse's stalls outlining which blanket to be used for what degree weather, which foot gets which little bootie, which supplements are administered on which weekday; the kind who will tell you five hundred different ways your horse can come up lame, or even juicier, dead. I like to avoid such detailed information. I prefer a comfortable membership in the horse-health-half-wit-society—when you know too much about a subject, such as horse health, the number of things that can go wrong will torture you.

I am fairly certain which horse it was that clocked Allie but thought it judicious to declare the incident an act of terrorism—given the current global atmosphere and the fact that I was quite fond of the owners of all three of Allie's field-mates.

The vet, after observing the injury and studying the initial x-ray, glibly announced that the situation was not "immediately euthanize-able"—heart-warming words. But, she added, Allie would have to be confined to her stall for many months on a limited diet, a regimen, she warned, that could very well "alter her personality considerably." You can safely interpret this to mean: create a pent-up, anxiety-ridden monster that you will likely regret had not been "immediately euthanized." Grim is too rosy a synopsis of this prognosis.

For those unfamiliar with the world of horse health, I should explain that the greatest danger in a situation of this type is with the accompanying, weight-bearing leg. In other words, the injury to her left hind leg posed the greatest threat to the right one, which now bore twice the weight. On a certain day in September the great race commenced between Allie's two hind legs, or more simply, between life and death. If the injured leg didn't heal in time, the weight-bearing leg would deteriorate and Allie would be "ultimately euthanized."

AT THE time of writing this book, I have witnessed the planned passing of scores of animals connected to our farm and surrounding neighborhood, all of which I have heartily endorsed. These animals have included horses, cats, dogs, piglets, lambs and deer, most of them ancient and suffering, some just suffering.

Knowing that I see death as a transition from one state of living to another and do not fear being present during the final hour, neighbors and fellow horse owners will often ask me to accompany them when they must make the difficult decision to help an animal to cross through death's door.

So convinced am I of the glory beyond this earthly life that I have occasionally visited my philosophy on neighboring wild animals and will often launch fierce prayer campaigns for the poor suffering creatures.

THERE IS nothing that so rattles my faith as the suffering of an animal. The witness of physical pain is horrible enough, but when psychological suffering is added, when the pain is due to the insensitivity of humans, which it too often is, when the animal is beaten, tied up, caged, overburdened, captured from the wild and forced into solitary confinement, and then neglected, the sight is excruciating. I have been known to rail against the one who orders this universe, hurling insults and threats.

C.S. Lewis suggests that God would rather suffer our rage than our indifference. I suspect he's right.

Of course, not all suffering is due to human ignorance. Some occurs naturally, and when this is the case, I am completely mystified. "WHY? Why would this be allowed by a loving God?" I implore, as I stare down the teacher. Oh, the poor, patient teacher.

BEFORE ALLIE was kicked, perhaps a year before, there was a doe in our neighborhood with a freshly broken leg. I presume this was the result of a collision with a car. In the natural order of things, no wild animal would have to live a compromised existence, because a predator would come and take its body. As I have mentioned, I don't believe it is possible to take an animal's spirit.

The reason this doe was still alive was that all of her natural predators in my area of the country have been eradicated, leaving my little doe to drag herself through a lonely existence without relief. Our human system of deer management is cruelly flawed. It allows, for one brief season, hunters (ranging from the proficient to the highly inebriated) to remove the finest specimens from the gene pool and leave the wounded and maimed. Nature would do just the opposite. It would take the wounded and weak and allow the robust to flourish. I look forward to the time when our strategies of animal management will change. Since I have been on the planet, I have seen signs of change. There are countries whose enlightened policies around this issue have had a huge effect on animal populations. Botswana banned all game hunting only five years ago and the positive effects have been surprisingly swift in coming, with the noticeable increase in animal populations and the calm that the animals have already begun to adopt toward humans.

When I first spotted the injured doe in my neighborhood, I indulged in a passionate argument with the teacher. We have had many such squabbles over the years. They usually go something like this: "Ok, I know we've messed up the system, we're idiots, but couldn't you just put this one out of her misery? I mean, aren't you supposed to be omnipotent, for goodness sakes?" Somewhere during this monologue, the doe turned to disappear in the wood, allowing me a view of her hind end, and oh my, I saw something truly awful. There was a mass protruding from her, a thing quite large, perhaps some internal organ. Well, that did it. I was now furious with whomever it is that orders the universe. The one whom we are told is the great lover of all beings! Every surety was suddenly unsure. Every ounce of trust threatened to abandon me. I was incensed.

"How could this be allowed?!" I thundered.

The deer passed into the woods but I thought of her constantly, and whenever I did, I pleaded for a hasty transfer into the next world where she might be whole again.

A couple of days later I saw her again—not so strange, as deer tend to stay within a small area, arriving at nearly the same time in the same neighboring places. This time I was able to inspect her more closely. Her leg was indeed very badly broken, never to be used again, and, horrible discovery, the object, which was still protruding from her, was not an internal organ, as I had suspected, but an unborn fetus. I'm sorry to have to write these words, they are so awful.

I launched into a fresh campaign of haranguing. "How? How? How, could this be allowed to continue?!! This is absolutely unacceptable! I want no part of a system that would allow such suffering."

And then the dreariest thoughts were unleashed, thoughts I hardly ever allow audience. "Perhaps the ones who say this life is just a cruel play of random chaos are right. How else could such misery be tolerated?"

For several days I was boiling with frustration. I'm not sure anyone noticed. I calmly called my friends in the area who hunt (the responsible types, the ones who will pass up the trophies to give relief to the wounded). Keep your gun handy, I told them, in case you see her. I'd given up on the game commission long ago. "Can she drag herself around to feed?" I'd been asked once when I reported a deer in my yard with a broken back. "I'm sorry ma'am, it's out of season."

I hadn't realized there was a season on mercy.

"Oh yeah, I've heard of that before," said a neighbor when I told him about the fetus, "eventually it'll just rot off." I was nearing the lunatic phase. I had visions of driving up to Canada and smuggling in a pack of wolves.

I had to calm down and think.

I met a woman once who told me that when she was a child she fell and hit her head badly and blacked out. "I spoke to God," she told me.

"And what did he say?" I asked.

"That the timing of our passage out of this world and into the next is more up to us than we think."

Oh, how I wished I could have a word with my doe.

I WOULD like to say that this story transpired over a matter of days but it was more like a week or two. Whenever I didn't see the doe I would grow hopeful, and then I would spot her, and my mood would go crashing to the ground. One day I spied her walking across a field while I was driving home. She was alone, as usual—an added cruelty. The inability to keep up with her kind is very difficult for a herd animal.

I was about to launch into my list of "How could

yous!" when she crossed the road just ahead and stepped off the blacktop. She then stopped, turned toward me and seemed to wait. I pulled up next to her, and instead of bounding off, my doe stood statue-still. It was chilly and my window had been closed. I pushed the button to lower the glass—an action that would have caused any other deer to leap for cover—but she remained, politely waiting for the window to reach the level of the door. I was so close to her that I could have reached out and stroked her rough coat, scratched her behind the ears. She looked into my eyes with a calm and, I thought, expectant gaze.

"You must leave this world." I said in a bold, no-nonsense tone. "This isn't a life for you," I continued. "I know you are going somewhere very beautiful. I know this. You must decide to go, decide today, and go."

She continued to listen, staring directly into my eyes, as I repeated, "You must decide to go now, you must." I stopped speaking, I had made my point, and we remained watching each other, our eyes unwilling to break their connection. Perhaps my conviction took a few moments longer than my words to enter her understanding.

She finally blinked, turned, and moved into the woods.

I never saw her again. I knew I wouldn't.

MY SISTER-IN-LAW'S twin sister was married to a man who worked in the military's special services. He was tough and taciturn, carrying military secrets to his deathbed. Near the end of his life the couple adopted a dog, a little fluffer-nutter, poodley thing. They named her Baby. Baby was utterly in love with this military man, and when, after six years or so of her life with this couple, the man developed brain cancer, Baby would not leave his side, sleeping on the pillow next to his head. A week before this man died, in the middle of the day, Baby, for no reason that anyone could determine (she was in fine health), died on the pillow next to him.

I believe she wished to be there to greet him when he crossed over a week later. I have heard of similar stories of animals dying either just before or just after their beloved human beings die.

One year a friend brought two feral cats to the barn. The cats had been fed for years outside her office building. The office was relocating, and these two kitties needed a home. The farm took them in and they lived in and around the barn for about two years. There is a room in the barn that is always kept above fifty degrees. The room is filled with cat beds and provides a very nice life for a feral cat. One of these two cats was ancient, near twenty years old, and the other was perhaps seven. They were inseparable friends.

One day one of the girls that helped out at the farm told me that the ancient kitty was looking poorly, and to be on the ready to get the call to drive her to the vet's office to help her to depart the world. I thanked her for the heads-up and waited for the call. The call came the next day, but it was not what I expected. The girl, choking back her tears, told me that one of the cats had suddenly died. "But," she went on to say, "It wasn't the old cat, it was her friend, the young one. She just died, for no reason, she just fell over dead." I ran over to the barn to gather the cat and we buried her on our property.

The next day I had another call from this girl. "You won't believe this but the old cat just died. She just died." I ran over to the barn to gather the ancient one and we buried her next to her friend. They died within twenty-four hours of each other.

I believe that animals have no fear of death. One reason for this is that they live too much in the present to fear the future, and furthermore, I suspect they may be able to see into the next world. Whenever I have had dream visits from my departed animal companions, there are usually other animals of mine, ones that are still alive, in the room with us, and they seem totally aware that the sprit animal is visiting. I believe that when an animal chooses to leave this world and enter the next, the impulse is often prompted by attachment, or love. We had a three-year-old cat, Doodad, who ran away and never came back. I had a dream several weeks later in which I saw Doodad playing with a pile of kittens, presumably those from her litter. She looked up at me from her happy activity and acknowledged me, and the resumed her play. Her mother had been a feral cat who only had two kittens by the time I trapped the little feline family but I was told by the vet who treated the mother that there obviously had been several more among this litter who had not made it. Perhaps the pull of attachment to these brothers and sisters had prompted her early departure from this world. I cannot know this, but the idea of her being pulled by love is comforting to me. I have just learned from a friend that just days after her brother departed the world, two of his house cats followed him into the next world. One was quite old, but the other was young, in fine health. This could be viewed as either a result of desperate pining, or an impulse to follow a beloved friend. Love always wins, in my estimation.

I have always thought that if I could give one gift to my fellow man that this would be the assurance of the continuation of the soul beyond death, for both humans and animals, indeed all of life. Of course there are many who do not need convincing, but there are others who find the idea of death terrifying.

For centuries there has been the hope that we will one day prove that the spirit continues after the moment of death. Yet there may be good reason why the proof has not yet arrived. As much as I love a good near-death experience, I can appreciate why another might find these stories ludicrous, even distasteful. The idea of life being like a book, with a beginning, middle and an end has its comforts. Were we too ready to accept the continuation of the soul after its time in this dimension perhaps we would be tempted to hasten our transition. I must trust the teacher on this one. If we were absolutely sure of moving on, we might grow apathetic and not work to find healthy ways to live our lives on Earth.

Ten

FTER HEARING Allie's prognosis, I did the only thing I could think to do—I planned a massive prayer attack on the Heavens. Most often, when asking for something from the divine, I feel a measure of reserve, an awareness that there might be more pressing issues elsewhere. Of course I know this. If we dared to weigh our concerns for comparison, we might always find heavier issues than our own. "I'm not keeping you from anything, am I?" I typically wonder, "Don't let me stop you from answering someone else's prayer." On the issue of Allie's healing I never adjusted my supplication to the perceived weight. I needed help. As comfortable as I was with helping the wounded and terminal out of this world, I simply didn't have enough understanding of the situation to see in which direction this story might be headed.

And so we followed the regime of stall rest. When I say we, I refer to myself and my farm manager Sharon, who was thankfully not a member of the horse-health-half-wit society and could therefore be trusted to administer the necessary goods, such as advice and injections. We visited Allie every day for the first several weeks, shooting her with drugs, fussing over her wound, cleaning around her, cleaning her. I would stay long after the manager and boarders left the barn, pulling grass for Allie, feeding her by the handful, often pulling up a chair just to sit with her, talk to her, sometimes read to her.

Allie always seemed grateful for the attention, whinnying when I entered the barn. She would hobble over to her stall door to study my strange human ways, hang her head over my own when I sat in my chair, breathing the air around me, gentle, curious. Angel, the old arthritic barn cat, always stood by; the two animals would often touch noses, I assumed in sympathy for shared pain.

Occasionally friends would visit, send cards, call. One friend's grandchild drew me a happy picture of Allie and me and herself, all together in perfect health. I nailed it to Allie's stall.

The vet had predicted that after two weeks Allie would attempt to use the leg a tiny bit. The first two weeks moved along swimmingly and, just as expected, her leg began to straighten a tad and looked as if it were bearing a bit of weight. During the third week, after much fussing, hundreds of prayers, bushels of carrots, the system of nonaction appeared to be working. Allie was improving. One night that week I remember tucking into bed with what felt like a lightness of being. "Thank God," I thought, "Thank you, dear teacher, for all of your help. All of my nagging supplications have been heard and she is healing. Thank you, thank you, thank you."

The next morning I walked into the barn and discovered what looked to be a complete relapse. Allie's injured leg hung, seemingly lifeless underneath her, the ankle (ok, I know it's not called that) and hoof curled into an "S" shape, unable to handle even the lightest weight. She moved slowly with a wincing toe-touch around her stall.

This wasn't the first time that Allie and I had suffered a setback.

ONE DAY during our first year together I had found myself in a riding ring astride Allie while a trainer attempted to turn her into a horse for civilized riding, and me into a rider with a degree of control. Allie was bored in the ring that day, and I must admit I was as well. At some point, out of utter tedium, Allie refused to move at all. I tried some gentle prodding and clicking, but she wouldn't budge, so I upped the clicking and prodding to no avail. The trainer asked to have a go at getting her to move, as I was getting nowhere, and I dismounted to hand the reins to her. She mounted Allie, but still she would not move, at which point the trainer hopped off, pulled out a whip, and proceeded to visit a violent temper tantrum on my horse, whipping her on her hind end over and over while she screamed at her. Allie danced around, wide-eyed and terrified as I stood watching, paralyzed with horror.

After the trainer was done with her, she turned to me and said, "Sometimes you have to take a horse out in back of the barn and beat it."

I have thought about this scene hundreds of times, astounded at myself for not stepping in and saving my horse from this behavior, and horrified again by what I saw. The only explanation that I can offer is that in that first year of ownership I was convinced that nowhere in Bucks County and the surrounding areas was there anyone more ignorant than I about horses. I have since concluded that where there is love, there is intuitive knowledge, and that is often more than enough to direct us. I hope I will never make the same mistake again.

As a result of this day, Allie grew even more fearful of people, if this were possible, and more and more grateful and calm with me. The process of healing began again, as if from day one, or perhaps minus one, and crept ever so slowly toward relative tranquility.

Eleven

TWO YEARS before the damaging kick to Allie's leg I was distinctly warned of its coming. The circumstances were identical to those of the clobbering incident that crippled her. A month or so earlier, I had gone through a period of disengagement with the farm, and with Allie. I can't remember the details, but I do know that when I got the phone call that Allie had been hurt, I felt a stab of guilt around my lack of involvement. This initial injury was much less life threatening, requiring only a couple of weeks of daily care. It was caused by another horse kicking her leg and I presume that it was the same leg that suffered the later, major wound. At the time I knew that the incident was telling me not to separate from Allie and from the farm. It felt like a warning from the teacher saying, "Stay involved. Life is meant to be involving. Show up. Live your life!"

I did heed the warning, but only for a year or so, and then went back to my lifelong habit of withdrawal. The teacher's forbearance is immeasurable. I had been handed a very fine lesson, learned it for a while, and somehow managed to unlearn it.

I HAVE a friend who has just recently passed through the great door and into the next world.

We met in a little theater troupe while we were both in our late twenties. My husband and I nicknamed him Tab, after the actor Tab Hunter, because he looked a bit like him, and he was an actor at the time, but the similarity ended there.

Tab was jovial, kind, patient, with a gentle, open face, thick glasses and long lanky body. He was loved by everyone in the company for his kind, easy-going nature. He was also known for his willingness to help close down the bar around the corner at the end of every night of the season, and I assume every night out of season. I understood that the schedule had been in effect for many years before I met him and it continued for many more after I left the company.

Tab was never unpleasant while inebriated, always convivial, but when completely pie-eyed he had a penchant for daredevil maneuvers that often resulted in mad tightrope walks along the edge of the long narrow bar, miraculously executed in a line straight enough not to make him pitch off.

I was in this theater company for two years, and only visited this bar a handful of times but by the second year I had heard enough about Tab's late night shenanigans to be worried. We all cared about him, and wished he'd be more careful with his good self.

One night, many hours after I had seen him leave the theater, and after several hours spent in his second home (the bar), he managed to leave it bodily intact, walk the few blocks home, and tuck himself into his loft bed. Such had long been his regular routine, but in the middle of the night, in a deep sleep, he fell out of the bed and landed on his back on the edge of a desk just below. He hurt himself very badly and was noticeably shaken when he arrived at the theater the next evening.

That night, after the performance, I told him that I was concerned about him. I felt he was on the road to really hurting himself, and hoped that he would relinquish his job at the bar. "Let the bartender closeup the bar tonight, and go home," I suggested. I believe a few others of our troupe spoke to him as well. It didn't help. He wasn't ready to make the change. He was thirty years old. There was in Tab a certain misguided notion about the romance around the theater and its connection to heavy drinking. Tab wrote poetry and plays and related to such figures as Dylan Thomas and Tennessee Williams.

I left the troupe at the end of the season and only kept up with Tab sporadically. He moved out of town to work with a small theater company in central Pennsylvania. On Easter morning, three years after I left the company, Matt and I heard from a mutual friend that Tab had climbed a tree in the wee hours and fallen out of it. He was in the hospital, and our friend was waiting to hear further news.

I instantly despaired. Matt asked me why I was so glum. "He'll be ok, I'm sure," he said. "Why are you so worried?"

I knew. He had been warned. I knew this was bad.

Tab was thirty-three when he became paralyzed from the waist down and was confined to a chair. The injury was at the very place along his spine where he had hurt himself several years before. He had climbed high up in a tree at the end of a long night of partying, when he lost his grip and landed on the sidewalk below.

As contradictory as this sounds, the fall saved him, saved his connection to life. He ultimately ended up seeing the fall as a resurrection, aptly delivered on Easter morning.

His old connection to life had been fuzzy, it sputtered and blanked out. He threw booze at it every night and it withered. He had grown more and more cynical (something so very foreign to his nature). He was no longer gratefully engaged in living. Indeed he seemed to have come to the point of rejecting the gift of life.

As I have mentioned earlier, I have wrestled with a similar resistance to life. Mine is manifested in other ways, yet still, I could relate.

Tab's gratitude for life after recovery, when he was able once again to live on his own, was extraordinary. He was gracious, appreciative of the smallest things and doubly patient. More dependent on people after his accident, he loved them even more. He noticed the subtle beauties around him. He was fully engaged.

Please don't imagine that I am implying that this accident was a punishing act on the teacher's part. The teacher doesn't operate that way. Like any good instructor, he or she will take advantage of an opportunity for learning, but it is up to us to do our homework. Tab had several chances to change course. He finally did open himself to the lesson, and grew and grew like a well-nourished plant.

He lived twenty-eight years in his chair.

WHEN I was eight years old my grandfather was killed in a car accident while he was on a trip to Jamaica. He was sixty-four. Before he left for his trip he hugged me. I knew then to worry. He wasn't a hugger. He was of a different generation, the last in a long line of non-hugging W.A.S.P.S. We had been quite close. He was one of the few members of my family that were as silly over animals as I was, and we spent our time together with his four dogs, noodling around on his farm, inspecting his menagerie of farm animals.

Three days or so after he died, I was in my school lunchroom when my classroom teacher pointed to an owl outside the window, perched on the branch of a tree. I am not sure how it came to be, that in a lunchroom full of children, I was the only one to have the owl pointed out to her. I stood for a long time staring and staring at the animal. I somehow gathered that the owl was sent to me, and that it had something to do with my grandfather. Of course, my grandfather would have loved to have seen the owl himself, but it was more than that. I felt someone watching me watch the owl. I was comforted.

Since that encounter, I have associated the daylight sighting of an owl, or any unusual encounter with this nocturnal creature, with the passing of someone near to me. It was later in life when I was to discover that there are whole tribes and cultures that view the owl as a symbol of the passing of a soul, but that day, I simply knew that it was so.

Tab died of a heart attack late on an August Monday. He was alone when he died, his brother later informed me, and his lifeless body was found early Tuesday morning. The night that Tab died, Matt and

I were sitting outside in our backyard, watching the darkness creep in, and listening for the nightly chorus of insects to rise. We heard an owl in the distance, nothing unusual for this time of evening. We had been hearing her, a screech owl, for a couple of weeks around dusk. The darkness was increasing, punctuated with the occasional mournful whinny of the owl. We sat a while longer when we heard something neither of us had ever heard before. It was the very near and clearly distinct flapping of strong wings above our heads: flap, flap, flap, flap, flap, flap. It sounded as if it were no higher than seven feet above our heads. We could not see the bird, but knew it was an owl. By the sound of its wings it was larger than a Screech Owl, perhaps a Great Horned.

"Wow" I gasped, "have you ever heard that before?"

"No, never."

"Beautiful."

And, after a moment I thought to myself, "I wonder who is leaving us?"

We were told the next day.

SEVERAL WEEKS after Tab's death, my husband and I were talking about those whom we might have forgotten to inform of his passing, and thought of a man who had been in the theater troupe all those years ago. We had left New York City in the mid-nineties and had not kept up with him. "Oh yes, he should be told," I said.

We came up with his first name, but struggled for a while with the surname. Eventually we arrived at it, but unfortunately, his last name was Smith. How were we to find this man with such a common name, especially in New York City, if he had indeed remained in the city?

That weekend I was scheduled to meet my old friend Boo for lunch in New York. We met in the village in Washington Square Park, and walked around from there, meandering, finding a spot for lunch, and moseying back to the square for a sit down and a chat before I was to get back in the car to head home. We were sitting for about fifteen minutes when a man walked past me who looked vaguely familiar. Suddenly it hit me, and I dashed up behind him, and stopped him. It was our old friend Mr. Smith. We enjoyed a long satisfying reminiscence about Tab and our time together in the theater troupe. He had been told of Tab's passing and it was a pleasure to reunite. I hadn't seen this man for 30 years.

This was the second meeting orchestrated with such fine precision during one of my rare and brief visits to the City. The other encounter had been with another member of this theater troupe, a young woman who had left the theater company the same year as I had, and who had gone on to attend medical school.

Knowing that my mind is useless when it's racing, my vision a blur, the teacher will play all sorts of tricks, perform all manner of stunts to get me to slow down. Obstacles will be tossed in my path, birds will fly will-nilly into my car windshield, shoes will disappear as I'm headed out the door, lists will vanish, dogs will throw up. I have come to suspect, when I am being particularly waylaid along my daily journey, that I am either being spared an uncomfortable situation or buttonholed for a significant revelation. The latter often transpire during chance meetings, meetings that would not have occurred, had I not spent an hour and a half dragging the front yard for my car keys.

One day while on my way into New York City from my home in Pennsylvania, I suffered at least fifty-five pesky delays as I headed out the door. This postponed my arrival to close to two hours later than I had planned. I was going to the Upper East Side— not my usual stomping grounds—and decided to park in a remote garage, farther away from my destination than I had intended. After parking, I thought I'd take a roundabout route down Madison Avenue for absolutely no reason that I can fathom in retrospect, except to cause myself even more delay. I was several blocks into my walk when I spotted the reason behind the hindrances. My old friend, the actress turned medical professional, who I hadn't seen for fifteen years, aimlessly crossed the street in front of me, stepping directly into my path. If I hadn't stopped, we would have cracked skulls. The circumstances of our parting and subsequent years of separation had been unfortunate. We had been quite close at one time and then torn apart by the difficult dynamics among a circle of friends. I believe both of us regretted having lost touch. We embraced, partly due to our nearly crashing into one another, and stood on that noisy corner joyfully catching up on our lives. Learning that she had moved off the island to Brooklyn, and was now a busy doctor, I asked her what the likelihood was of her being in that part of Manhattan in the middle of a weekday. The answer was just shy of zero, and I could almost claim the same odds myself.

In the case of both encounters, with this friend and with Mr. Smith, when I try and imagine the complex maneuverings behind these meetings, the overtime that the teacher must have put in to cause these reunions, I am astounded.

I saw a documentary once about mind control. It attempted to prove that we, as individuals, are the sole creators of our lives. The buck stops here (point to own chest). One man claimed that he woke up every morning and planned his day from morning to night, and went on to say that his day never deviated from this predetermined course. He maintained that he was always in absolute control of all the circumstances of his life. My main concern with such a notion is, why? Why would one wish to so hinder the teacher? Why miss out on all of the spontaneity, mystery, surprise and possible awakening? Can you imagine the colos-